(flood basement

Caitlin Press Inc.
8100 Alderwood Road
Halfmoon Bay, BC, V0N 1Y1
www.caitlin-press.com

Cover design by Shannon Reece.
Text design by the house.
Caitlin Press would like to thank Erin Schopfer for her exemplary editorial assistance.
Printed in Canada.

Caitlin Press Inc. acknowledges financial support from the Government of Canada through the Book Publishing Industry Development Program and the Canada Council for the Arts, and from the Province of British Columbia through the British Columbia Arts Council and the Book Publisher's Tax Credit.

Canada Council   Conseil des Arts
for the Arts   du Canada   BRITISH COLUMBIA
                                           ARTS COUNCIL
                                           We acknowledge the support of the Province of British Columbia
                                           through the British Columbia Arts Council

Library and Archives Canada Cataloguing in Publication

Stewart, Jeremy, 1982–
    (flood basement / Jeremy Stewart.

Poems.
Title is preceded by a parenthesis.
ISBN 978-1-894759-34-2

    I. Title.

PS8637.T49455F56 2009   C811'.6   C2009-900722-3

(flood basement

Jeremy Stewart

Caitlin Press

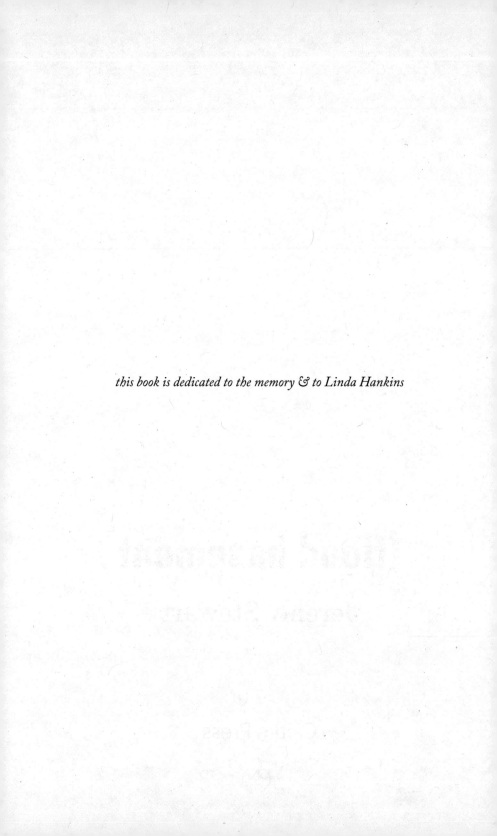

this book is dedicated to the memory & to Linda Hankins

one

(flood basement

the hood

(spray-painted in black on the back wall
of a gas station in an alley at the edge
of the Veteran's Land Act / Van Bow area)

9

Fort George Park is half graveyard   half love letter
to working mothers and blonde babies
        stoned long-hairs   as my Grandpa would call them
        melted ice cream & discarded condoms
        an old fellow with his shoes off

                                        gazing out over the Fraser
        me and my friends   deceased and alive
        victorious drag queens
        Archie from Fort & his wife Edith & their daughter Gloria (in that order)
        the ghosts of the Lheidli T'enneh
from our "pioneers" / "settlers" / "founding fathers"

& when I was on a kindergarten field trip there
I saw a yellow eye on a spruce
that could see me

a sentinel of the ghosts of the Lheidli T'enneh
a witness for the ghosts of the Lheidli T'enneh

& I was so convinced it was real
I can remember it

I often attempted to look for the eye later   but as I grew

                                        the forest
                                                    shrunk
until there was nowhere left to find

search that one path down
                        to the river's edge
smoked my first full cigarette there
                                sick and powerful
                                        / dizzy and proud

the concrete remains of a mystery road
used to prevent the bank's erosion   in vain

kissed Erin there in the summer dusk   embraced
fell in the sand   dropped her camera
cried and looked upside down at the tracks
                                              across the brown Fraser water

the hardness of the muddy Fraser water
antifreeze-green by nightfall
                              like the time we were propositioned
                              "you boys should come back with me
                              to my girlfriend's"
                              by a middle-aged Native man
                              at midnight on LSD riding
                              the red fire engine
                              "no thanks"

                              hallucinating in the dark   the girl
                              was a lizard   hahaha then
                              being escorted out by the security man.
                              Purple haze aura enshrouded
                              the zombie city.   Psychedelic surgery
                              lacerates the heart of the knife juggler.
                              The sad clown points to his face
                              and   wiping it away   reveals a shadow

I sang here
the ghosts of the Lheidli T'enneh
                              beyond my vision

          (you ever been to a sweat lodge? No

at daycare at age six I sang the song from the Native TV show in the concrete
tube in the breezeway and Stella (a real live Native) said it sounded Carrier

11

whose ghosts are these
               that I raise?

                          A haunted playground
                          a whitewashed school

the eminent local historian (Rev.) F.E. Runnalls:
                          "their religious beliefs
                          were primitive

                          some notion of a divine being
                          that controlled the world
                          through the agency of spirits"

                / and who will prepare the medicine?

once L. and I
met on Royal Crescent
I'm riding my bike   I've taken several laps around
the block   where L. and I live
at our respective houses (quiet   yellow afternoon   distant Queensway buzz

they saw me out the window
him and B.

I ride too hard   or something   the chain falls off
I begin to walk my bike home.
B. comes up riding his bike with L. doubling on the handlebars
I'm looking into a puddle in the gravel   no curb here
the sun is sparkling through the water

L. rides by   kicks me in the shoulder   laughs hard
B. and him veering all over the empty road   back for another pass
I grasp the situation quickly   nothing to do but keep walking
my bike home   kicked again   again   laughter
they take off. At home, I scream at my mom and sister, get a kitchen knife
to go kill L. and B.   I stay home instead
throw the knife at the porch   ricochets
almost hits my sister (three-years-old). There is no rescuing this

(20th Ave., 7-11 parking lot)

I was not
found dead in the 7-11. I was found in
the parking lot

I was found out
in the parking lot of the 7-11
dead.

Winter aggregates on the ground, aggravating people
sleeping there behind the 7-11, wind-assaulted
alive, wired like crows, freezer-burned and black

coughing, spasmodic frost heaves, heavy breaths, under
their BC Medical, their Premium Fair Pharmacare
unavailable, the medicine men living off the avails

stark weak trees sick and naked, wrapped
in the white lights like razor wire, celebrate
the coming of the millennium, installed by civic authorities

faded asphalt lined with creases like palms, cupping the spilt
coffee-stained sweatpants of our secret neighbours
gasoline more than a smell, more than it's ever been, dearer

TELUS pay phones no one wants to touch, except the man
who swallows the receiver and chews his words
in a hollow mouth black with a chaw of Redman snoose

mummified
in a grey wool Woolworth's
floor-length women's winter coat

I lay me down to sleep
now, I'm being harangued
they're pulling off my shoes (my soles to keep)

eyes found me right justified and sans serif
not in the 7-11, but outside, always
keeping my hands in my ripped-off pockets

my language a modulation of the wrappers
"may contain traces of partially hydrogenated
modernist tradition" now lying in the parking lot

cast-off and outworn, a recycled bicycle under
the wheels of a new F-350, sparks flying little
children swearing in the magazine aisle, looking on

burnt garbage for warmth, rearranged remains
found, left-bracketed but not right, unfinished
and though they blast Indian classical, I am inexorable

a raspy throat crows a hoarse cry

                                    /   calls out:

wire birds sing the day before a black cloudburst
/ descant with ghosts

                          who will not answer

this is my street
so I sing along

city of long shadows

city of long shadows

city of long shadows

city of long shadows

multiple exposed
images of street
                    cracks in the side
                                    walk down to where
the sun has leverage.
Balancing on a celestial fulcrum
                                    we cannot see
the Earth
            irrevocably over-
                            exposed

footsteps like simplified
breakbeats punctuated by pebbles
rustling against pavement under soles

4/4 pattern in the step
sequencer   day's last light oblique
and liquid on black puddle surfaces

rocks beatbox a square wave
a river ripple quavers a hymn
language out of range on the shortwave
clearer than the Nechako

I don't need headphones to hear music

random
across the road

PATRICIA SUBSTATION
                            THE GATEWAY
                                            PETRO-CAN

the lyrics
into the wind   the mind   the wind
a Cottonwood Island of the Mind
Ferlinghetti's ferris wheel's
electric lights rendered
mute   static
a low trumpet solo bathed in television snow
an omnichromatic electronic orchestra
broken like Philip Glass
on the Nechako

undermixed and haloed
digital song   listless
breath blown through cottonwood leaves
to the mill just beyond the Nechako
the mind blown by the wind
        a loose fitting
                        binary opposition
        the organic and the imaginary
                searching the gravel lot to find
                imaginary numbers in nature

between the ecstatic and the ideal

        headlamps on a blue firebird light up

once L. and I
met, at my house, his cousin B. was there
I was eating a slice of processed cheese
B. asked for one, I went in the house, I went in the fridge, I got him one,
I went back out, he was still there, I gave him it, he didn't
say thank you (later, my mom says, "you had bloody well better not be
feeding those little bastards
we'll never get rid of them" I didn't lie. She swore)
L. punches me
in the stomach at the end
of the alley behind my house. B. and him laugh and laugh.
I go back in. I cry. I'm just a white kid
with glasses. I'm fair game.

pg is going
to suck

(black felt pen on the electrical box
across from the bank building at 6th and Victoria)

(7th Ave, Legion Hall parking lot)

LC Gunn Park is haunted.
The boys and I chain smoke
Dunhills in a rusted green
'79 Cougar. Night never turns black
in the month of July, at two AM it's still
midnight-blue. Haze rising from the mill shrouds
sickly orange light and hell. Metallica pounds out
our soundtrack like it was 1989, not 1998

       long dark hair and denim

We wield our dreams, welded together from scraps
found out in the yard. Rock n' roll burns
holes in our shirt sleeves. This is the end
of thinking that we weren't wrong about jobs
and school. We won't still remember that
next year. Our girlfriends will want us
to get our own places. Us boys will conform
and shave our grimy little beards, etc.

       long dark hair and denim
       double-kick drums and floor toms

"Denny's is the shore on which
the dregs of humanity washes up," I announce
in error. Note the full soap dispenser. The muddy
Fraser could be that same bank, at Paddlewheel Park
where our four fathers played rock,
paper, scissors for our three mothers. We cut in
when Workers' Comp still let us have a puff. We buy coffee
and sit up until dawn, when we butt out

long dark hair and denim
double-kick drums and floor toms
tremolo picking down-tuned XLs

Handing out handbills from the tables, the kids
all want to be there on September 13th. We don't mind
getting kicked out for soliciting. The waitress is rude, but
she gets our bills right. The Legion show is coming
together. Subversion, Negative Aggression, Dead
Reckoning; I scream and play lead
in Telepathy. We headline. When three hundred tickets sell,
we make ourselves sick with the money

long dark hair and denim
double-kick drums and floor toms
tremolo picking down-tuned XLs
slap-back drenched garage howls
2x15 bass cabs with horns
black Marshall stacks and heads
stereo QSC 2000 watt amps
mosh pit injuries and unsigned waivers
sudden flood of angry cops come up
drunk kids fucking in a hatchback
with an audience of cheering skids
moustachioed pigs pepper spray
little punk pissing on a van
"Security" man smokes the most weed
hey, that guy's got a dead tooth
saw a flying saucer from the parking lot
51-year-old man borrowed his mom's
car hitting on a 15-year-old girl

dusty portrait of the Queen on the wall
behind the band smiles unperturbed
the metal Growl For Meat contest
blows the PA all to hell
stereo QSC 2000 watt amps
black Marshall stacks and heads
2x15 bass cabs with horns
slap-back drenched garage howls
tremolo picking down-tuned XLs
double-kick drums and floor toms
long dark hair and denim

watercolour clouds   cartoon bus victims
in plastic sunglasses   mirrored
a day without sun
brakes squeal and potholes lurch

      an academic youth
      denies the love of a gas station girl

      a tribute to reality TV

      eyes won't see the ghosts
      in the apartment's parking garage
      hear how they hiss
                to one another of burning
                polyester and summer
                        colds

three men sit on the liquor store steps asking for change
the lawyer reasons: "why not just cut out the middle man
buy them a bottle"

parking spaces / hard white lines decaying
unbroken pavement   beneath
the street light day   a squalid imitation
a starved moon shining its high beams into the eyes of strangers
white faces in a convenience store lineup

asphalt on the blood / hard sodium lights   abrade   permeate
my narrowing spectrum   an incandescent spectre   no blue or
green photons—an orange shadow. The eye corrects
    twelve percent grey

small stones set in tar

once L. and I
lived on blocks of Regents Crescent divided by Rose Lane
where my brother and I took boards
from Canadian Custom Countertops back lot
without asking to build our very own fort in mom's backyard
without asking. L. helped us
put dozens of unnecessary nails in each board
my friend Flip helped, too. We were going to have a club. We didn't want L.
to help. We thought he laughed like a girl.

When it was half-finished, my beloved
Grandfather decided it was condemned
he demolished our fort with one
push. We built a new one soon

third breakdown in as many days

roadside gravel is dusty   to sit on   kneeling
                        brown rusty fender red
                                        light fading too fast over
the horizon through the scrawny lodgepole pines   green   blackening

"I'm on my way
            to Canaan land
  I'm on my way
            to Canaan land
  I'm on my way   oh yes
            to Canaan land
  I'm on my way
            glory Hallelujah
                        on my way"

                                        MOTEL: a lit sign
standing at the edge of Highway 16 again   waiting on a lift
back down   the headlights just won't turn on at all
Erin's in tears here now   O LORD

big round rocks like I'd use
to throw at anybody who came over here to hurt her
get my hands dirty
                                        release us.

Subdivision

        a grey Ford turning left in there has a passenger with a baseball cap
        gives me a long look   come on

my uncle drives up in a silver car to carry us home

Erin: "when I heard you singing, I laughed
and cried at the same time"

**death
to
geeks**

(black felt marker on the wall of a bookstore
and café, in the doorway of a defunct sports bar)

escaped from school following another little breakdown
just ran away   left incredulous authority figures slack-jawed
not chasing me through the snow   to the road; newly spring dry
& cold. Wet sock   gravel grinding in   where in hell am I going (?

           Institutional life as recurring nightmare)

I get all the way up Moss Ave to the highway, where I knock on a duplex door,
a mother woman is persuaded to let me use the telephone to call my mom
at work, she doesn't know what I want her to do! I start to head home

I get all the way up to the top of the Jasper Ave hill when the principal rolls
up smiling mildly in his '70s boat car, picks me up, and takes me
to my mom's house   doesn't say a word

it's unsettling   how this dust has settled
South Fort has shifted little since sepia antiquity
Rose Lane—not even the name has changed

once behind the locked door I am safe. Now pours forth the lament
a six string electric crying jag   a flooded basement
daylight flooding through the ground level windows of a ruined day

a short suspension   a counselling session
a colour television   tension
I want everything to go right right now. Please

(street lamp buzz)

orange street lamps speak low
zzzzzzzzzzzz
in their sleep
they make snow pink now
pink street lamps make the snow seem candy sweet
white street lamps are coldest / calculating a murder scene / your movements
made mechanical zzzzzzzzzzzz
blue street lamps / night flowers bloom solarized
transport you into a gegenlichtaufnahmen movie frame of mind.
Yellow street lamps rot the teeth out of your skull.
They turn on when you walk by

they burn out when you walk by.
They know to wake up in the morning and hang
out waiting for the bus.
They know to snore
they are friends to traffic
signals and walk figures.
They know to not work all the time.

Postscript.
zzzzzzzzzzzz

(Lamp) post-postscript.
zzzzzzzzzzzz

once L. and I
met suddenly when him and B. leapt out of the tall grass
on the Heritage Trails. I'm walking home from Fort George
Park with Jon and Flip when the grasses rustle
and they come screaming
AAAAAAH
out. They run
up to us, ten feet away, and stop, panting. I say, you guys
sure are tricky. They say it's 'cause they're Indians. There's hostility,
(They're Hostile! They're Restless! They're On the War Path!
They're A-Gonna Scalp Us! Call In the Cavalry!)
I feel it, but there's two of them and three of us.
I hate fighting.
I wish they would die.

Someday.

Eyes speak filmic speechlessness
turn   in   the snow
come to   know (see   speech for the eyes
cinematography of posture and breath
mute darkness, or   sound that conveys a gesture
the hand that gently wrings   the neck
                                        of the violin
ceaselessly reading a break
                            into the line

red tail lights a bare branch a broken glass
holes in the moon a stop sign a turn signal—
    frost a pay phone a brown shroud of exhaust cloud
a white clearcut a held hand a fog window,
(horns, a green belt, a black wire above us
gas station bell, a penny found, a townhouse

and that's our show!

Windshield wipers and dashboard-light reflections wash across
eyes. Eyelids drop
                        a rain instant
        under water   the rail
                permeated
                                by the driving
                                        like rain
                                                drops into the Fraser
from the grey concrete height of the Yellowhead bridge
into negative dreams and 16mm grain in low light
bluing, saturated   numb lips & speedometer numbers
blur under / over wavering
                                radio frequencies and the sound
        static

the south side of the river
brake lights spark defocused circles / small red
eyes crave sleep and drive

a sigh heaves
fogs up glass
                                fingers find words to erase
from the surface

(train whistles somewhere beneath us
    going home tonight

if you read this your gay/lesbo

(in felt pen on the wall behind a gas station)

(Queen of the Queensway Drag Queens)

RIP

F----- (F---) P-------

you were the Queen, alright, you were so damn hot
people didn't even know you were Queen

and on a damn cold morning, when they were opening up
you were found out in the alley

the papers couldn't print the news, but the word
got around downtown, a legend by sundown

the Big Man was wasted after a visit to the Columbus, and damn
if the peelers didn't work him up a hankerin'

Queensway autumn black and lamp-orange October wind unwound
the window to pick up a faux fur long bleached hairdo stranger, baby

the Big Man took the Queen for a ride, the Queen took the Big Man
for a ride, and who knows just how far they got together

the Queen, a shocker, street-walker, smooth-talker, the Big Man got more
than he bargained for, but he was prepared to cut a deal

that was the coldest, hardest, ugliest winter
the city had ever known.

An electric light dream   midnight pupils learning   curves of Queens
way down a steep dive   on a decay-ridden twelve-speed

a hard concrete lesson   unlearnt   no skull caesura necessary
discouragement mixes medicine for ignorance

mercurial approach tempered by weather   heavy metal / washed out
eye blue / faded denim   heart chasm   come cross me

and sometimes   while riding home, I   would stop watching
where I was   going down
                              the hill   Now Entering Historic
                    SOUTH FORT GEORGE
tearing past   this sign I don't see   but know   and I would feel
the sidelong drift
toward the guardrail / quickly look. Not now
                              almost fail to turn.

                              Cold wind / loud ears.

A lonesome silver drone
                              buzzes into the night sky / an arc lamp fly
metallic taste   black summer pavement   rap bass blasting
open neighbourhood air   highway hums by my bedside
pregnant homeless cats   & grass growing up inside
aggravated sinuses

tenuous threads weave between
                              fence posts
paint peeled to reveal weathered wood

an inverted shopping cart
                        submerged in the soft wet brown

when the slough snow dump melts, there will be coins
to find. Brother Jon and I, as children,
scour this dirt forever.

Reclaim street names

a fall from a bike
                  at the foot   of the Hudson's Bay Slough
trails. (Heritage Trails— whose, exactly?)

                                    blue / green
weeping birch leaves shiver in the wind
& between the blue and blue-green
                                    physicists' axioms fall
before mine: distances increase
                  while running to escape
                  the driving rain

                        oh, it's really coming down now

"you're the greatest tripper who ever trupp"
said blonde hairdo boy
who piloted the brown 1980 Ranger through the crescents
and parked it in the gravel parking lot behind the shop wing

(where the skids smoke their orange bud   "lumbering dicks": because
once they grew up, like their dads,   they would work in forestry (hence:
lumber   and they walked like "lumbering" + they were dicks named
Richard / cock and balls type / roosteresque pseudochimp milldudes

us selling grass   getting high   (enough to assassinate characters from above
& in the mall back lot   chain smoking unfiltered Camels 100s
the signs are so bright   we are in a plastic hell
(how many times through hell   how many hells

Satan recognising the freshness of pain in variation
/ the hell of our own selves' variation   who now to expect?
After a run-in with the infamous fan pipe forgetting my own face
finally finding the mirror: "oh, it's *you* again"

take sanctuary in the Sears Country Inn (behind the stairs down to it
so ripped we could see the door to space   (outer space, that is
but how can we go through it? Locked.
Drank coffee black   sitting across the cafeteria
from Barry McKinnon and John Harris   unbeknownst to us
laugh now   a secret convergence of poets
hidden even from them   (McKinnon writing *The Centre*
& me writing heavy metal lyrics   "this is a song called Beard of Bees"

in night parks   feeling cold
lighting Zippos in the wind
denim jacketed and long-haired   blonde boy in his white bandanna
    Creeping Death Weed (after the Metallica song from 1984)
purchased in a garbage bag from Hells Angels at a concert in Vancouver
thrown in the trash by mom and dad who tape recorded his phone calls

his girlfriend threatened suicide   (let her do it (can't stop
her   control freak   probably
doesn't even want you   to be in a band
cancel the show   anyway   change our names

              blonde hairdo boy drew a picture of me hanging myself
sideways
    finally faded out
staring into the coloured lights
                              "no you"

        ghosts
                ephemeral, drifting through
                                        concrete places
        ghosts
                concrete within
                                ghostly places
        the Yellowhead bridge
                        at night   witness
                                        a cloud rising
mill glowing All Saints' orange
reflecting on the bloody Fraser
                        how many bodies over the rail?

                                        Heavy with toxic breaths
the Yellowhead bridge angles through
a rail of ghostly concrete

The Galaxy

we love you always
"J---- L------"

(The Galaxy was a teen nightclub, now closed down.
The name on the old Galaxy building's wall, omitted here,
belonged to a young aboriginal man who committed suicide
because of the social persecution he faced
as a homosexual)

fag

(this was written on top of the words above
in red permanent marker)

> once L. and I
> walked up our street
> his cousin W. was standing in the middle, smoking
> he had long black hair, a backwards cap,
> a punched-out face. Maybe eighteen
> he says, "hey faggot

> (I don't look up. I just keep walking. I'm eleven.)

> "hey   faggot

> you fucking deaf?

> I'm talking to you

> yeah, you just keep walking. Don't fucking turn around, 'less
> you want to die."
> When I get home, I'm
> shaking
> L. says later,
> "Don't worry, man. When W.'s around, just don't be
> such a faggot."

(The centre of it all)

nothing is ready to happen
                    here

nothing is happening
              here
                    right now

and there will be nothing to listen to   so close
                    so listen close anyway, hear the highway in-
                    and exhaling
                    the ashen pallor of another
                    new subdivision

                    "we're so predictable, we are
                    perfect"

                    a white vinyl siding epidemic

          in the mall ("the centre of it all")
          this season's responses form
          a pattern flowering   a grand opening
          on the wall repeating
          questions to existing unexciting answers

enter the exits and cease to exist. Enter the exits and cease to exist.
Enter the exits and cease to exist. Enter the exits and cease to exist.
Last
left.

There's an abundance of nothing
                              to hear   if you listen

the still places in me resemble Cottonwood Island Park
away from the trail lines
                              into the entropic gloom
warm and creeping   fireweed
twilit

the still places in me resemble those spaces between the buildings
on Victoria Street
                        deadened by their own weight
                                      against the wind

the angel and the archaeopteryx fly together
                          / at the zenith /
                                the city is lit gold
                                w/ Mt. Zion glory

and I wear down my shoes here
at the azimuth
in the rain
           gutters
the shutter of my still camera blinking back the sun

and still   still   those places in me
reflect   between the axons & dendrites
on the possibility of a revelation

to hear the word in a dime I find on the corner of 3rd and Dominion

to break down
decompose   the black
                                        and white lines
                      on the sheet of news-
                                              print that lies
under the fallen poplar
                          leaves
                                    rotten beyond recognition
when the snow melts in
                              spring seeping
                                              sustenance from dead layers
into the green earth

that is the creative process
of a northern poet

once L. and I
crossed the South Fort George Elementary field in winter's belly, vision obscured
by hood and scarf, L. wearing no hood or scarf, looking
tough. In a bomber jacket, the little hood.
He sure swears a lot when he talks.

St. Valentine's, my first day
at South Fort George Elementary
by the end, I'm suspended for fighting
and swearing. I call a girl a bitch, I throw a desk
at the teacher, the principal wants to have a long chat

he talks slow.
This school is going to be the same

once L. and I
crossed the South Fort George Elementary field in rotten winter's
end and found
a weathered tablespoon. I ask, for a child's pudding? L. says
blow or smack for sure, don't fucking pick it up
(but it isn't burnt

I am the stoplight shadow
                    cast   red

I can't have the Highway 97 underpass back
kick dust into the eyes of approaching traffic

mall parking lot cars pinprick depression into this doll
                                        this candy heart

my shoes were born to erode the road
                born in the hands of a machine

a wide street for fat men in trucks
traffic congestion causes phlegm

under a spring flood
                    glory gutters in the sun
my jeans don't fit me anymore
                            and my socks are wet

(what I want to know is just how long can I stare out
these barred basement windows at the crows
on the power lines before I become one

as I fly
        black / feathered
                    above

could that be a
parka if it was worn
by a m̶ m̶ man of a very
small height Answer Yes but
it would be a very poor fitting
parka

(no. 2 pencil on the splintered wooden
door of a bar, now gone under)

went for a swim there once   with Noah

it rained white   the sun electrified every bolt
of water that drove through   our eavestroughs

he was crashing at my mom's. The blinds in our kitchen window
let in enough day to see that it was raining sheets
                                                  and then
                                        silence

cleared up
we figured it was time to go find a smoke. But my alley
was completely submerged

15th Ave was a creek   there were cars stalled all the way
downtown   where the flood was draining to
the library parking lot was a pond   some jackass in a truck
spinning his tires and raising water   everyone was laughing
a beautiful freak accident   and at the public pool
near the fountain   we found a wallet

but it was empty

we went home. No money   no smokes.

once L. and I
went into his parents spring-flooded basement
and he takes out a black box and a black lighter. The lighting is half
dead cold fluorescent.
The stale river-water smell is alkaline, incandescent in my nostrils.
He puts on Cypress Hill.
I want to hold my breath

once L. and I
found ourselves opposite
in his kitchen
when I was touring houses for sale with my mom and sister.
He ignored me and prepared an omelette
(our homes had the same floor plan

the smell hung on

kicked off
welfare
mob
Apr 1 04

(on the door of Chalky's, a pool hall now out of business
on notorious George Street, in reference
to the Liberal government's decision to withdraw
welfare support from a large number of citizens)

bums eat for free

(also on the door of Chalky's, in response
to the previous quote)

(lines for my famous father from the intersection of hwys. 16 and 97)

Mr. PG is my dad. Don't ask me
to explain how that works.
I'd blush.
He's tall   about twenty-seven feet
and bald   that's why he wears a hat
a hard hat   he works at the mill
he went bald from worrying about the economy.

I am his son. I have to be tough.

He's always waving the BC flag, or raising
awareness of Canadian blindness week or whatever
and asking people who pass by
the intersection of highways 16 and 97
if they've had their flu shot.
You might say he's a political activist.

He's made out of fibreglass and metal   painted
to look like wood.

I know   a lot of people say we look alike.

He's been around Prince George long enough to remember
the boom of '67. Not me. I didn't show up until the bust of '82. Don't talk
bad about it. That was the bust that nursed me.

There's a time capsule in his body. That's because he cares
about history   local matters   and
because he can't move   so he can't stop

kids from putting time capsules in his body. I feel for him.

He welcomes strangers and friends.

Some people don't like him. They say he's a hick
that he makes us look bad. They call him an eyesore
I'd like to see how they'd look   after thirty or forty-some years
standing at the intersection of highways 16 and 97.
He might be a little stiff   socially   but
if you knew him like I know him   you couldn't
get him to shut up.

When he wears those sunglasses   man   he's like Joe Cool.

He doesn't like the new neighbours. The casino? It's going to be noisy at night
there's going to be all kinds of snotty tourists making fun of him
as if he didn't have enough problems already   the pine beetles
didn't realise he'd been rebuilt of sturdier stuff
after he was torched by hoodlums
now the bugs infest his drawers   he says it's itchy

only kidding. He doesn't wear any drawers.

I, for one, am proud of him.

South Fort is taking on water
no one's left there to bail it out

my basement got an inch more every spring

my family finally floated away

& as I took a leak
over the fence
they sang:
Jeremy don't care
                    if his ass is bare
                                        and the wind goes whistlin'
                        through the hair

once L. and I
were hanging out at lunch
with the cool boys
there's a vacant house
in the cul-de-sac on La Salle
we go there
I stand outside, because I'm a chickenshit faggot, I guess
the guys break everything. You can hear the glass
all over, but nobody does, except
me. I say nothing. I sing to myself.
They do this every day for weeks.
I hear somebody pisses on the furniture, somebody
shits on a plate and puts in the oven.
The laughs just don't stop
you little fucks

I can escape
can I escape
can't I escape
I can't escape

(my own song "Schizophrenia": from 4th and George, downstairs)

in the Spy Market he told me
"your guitar playing will kill 'em all."
Skaface, we called him, after Ska punk
and because he had terrible acne scars. (a.k.a Sam from Nazko
now he was a guitarist and a half   punk rock
                                        and Stevie Ray Vaughan.
                                            "Nine years on guitar."

in the Spy Market   I played my first show
threw my guitar at my drummer   ran outside in the snow and ice
fourteen-years-old   little punk

in the Spy Market   when I saw Submission Hold
(fastest string change ever: the bass player broke his E
in the verse   and was in tune and playing by the chorus (drummer
detuned his toms; flapped like rubber bands (blue-haired female "singer":
                    SCREEEEEEEEEEEE!!!
Skaface and I were abusing an acoustic guitar after the show
        with some Victoria emo punks
I played my newest song   alternate tuning   melancholy
            that's when he said it. Those words haven't left me

Skaface was in love with Danielle   he looked at her
from across the courtyard   where the punks ate lunch
and botched skateboard tricks. They were mostly Jehovah's Witnesses' kids
rebelling. Many were named Justin. Mohawks / piercings / wrinkled clothes.
Non-smokers   (this is all at Prince George Senior Secondary
Danielle was a shy girl.   She and Skaface tried to talk to each other
(and somewhere   tumbleweeds went rolling by

I don't know what all went on with him and Danielle. I don't think it worked
out. But Skaface started smoking a lot of grass. He never did that before
but then he did. He started skateboarding too.   He seemed sad
somehow. Then I heard he became schizophrenic   went to live
in the Psych Ward   and then moved back to the reserve.

55

I tried to call him there   his parents were old
there was no reply.

In my memory I see him in the driveway on Petersen Road after we
jammed talking quietly about punk rock and revolution

I see him in the hallway in front of the orange lockers under half-dead
fluorescents with the redhead who was in his band (the Skexees) / who was
his girlfriend   for a while

in my mind I see the parking lot of the townhouses where my family lived
on the hill above the high school   under the blue light after a show
myself   long hair and jacket trailing behind in the night breeze
repeating his words in my mind—"kill 'em all"   too much.

Onstage with him at Fort George Park   singing myself raw for
Elizabeth
who was lying in a Prince George Regional Hospital bed
in an epileptic coma   dying

at the mall   waiting for the kid who wanted to fight me (Skaface
went home early; the kid showed up late
I kicked the kid's ass in front of his mom buying flowers. He was wearing
a swastika ring which left a mark on my right eyebrow

the kid was asking for it.)

In my memory I see his bedroom in Prince
where he played me Sonic Youth's "Schizophrenia"
on his stereo (I loved it. I stole the title for my own song

whatever happened to him.

(Sunday morning at the 5th Ave. Laundromat)

God calls out to you

above the rattle
              of buttons
                      in the unheard   silence
                              between

twin boys with hot wheels
                  and a welfare mom
a cascade of shiny quarters waiting to be plunked
the Indian matron with her ethereal orange clothes and braided black hair
the ashtray full
              of half-smoked
                      menthol 100s

a lonely sock

fluorescent grunge

God's voice
              beneath the machine hum

answer the ringing
              courtesy telephone

> once L. and I
> were in shoes on the hockey rink
> with the cool boys. We're the grade 7s.
> The little kids are playing with Power Rangers
> I take the fat kid's toy and smash it
> on the ice. I feel like the biggest
> asshole in the universe. The tough ones laugh
> like loons.

> I am suspended. I have to replace the doll. It's twenty dollars.
> My mom could kill me. The principal says it's the last straw. In three weeks
> I'm on correspondence
> I pay for it with my paper money.

> I'm made to apologize.

When the streets get dry, I'm going
under the snow, the promise of muddy
lawns springing up
                    see the gloom
                                  corrode

sepulchral white   stained alive
schoolyard seas parted by sunrays

my sneakers will bare my feet when worn
                                    through

from bedrooms out, leaving
like vines, green
and gold-flecked eyes
on a girl

revivified pasty faces in suburbia
spill   chlorinated and fluoridated
to moisten and swell the pages of this book
the ink runs
            from these words
                            into the air

morose and lachrymose   rows of pews
a pen and penance   a few words for dead ants
                                                beneath my shoe.

The ants
            tunnel
                    holes
                            in the ground
the ants
            dream in mono-
                    chrome
slaving away
            from their black hearts
                                    into their black
                                                lungs
yellow dust covers all
                    the things they build
                                    or destroy
a sick morning opens its clouds upon them
aspirin   violently   alkaline
                                        beneath my smile.

Smiled sadly and with long-suffering patience into my shirt
a stifled sob   a hard throat   a suppressed cough
a swallowed word   swallows in the rafters
shallow wallows in soul shoals   snickering at my passing pages

smiled slowly and with acid amusement into my shirt
a burnt paper   a smoking scrawl   poems into the graves of poets
gravel road grief   a typewriter for Sam
a weighted sigh   waiting on stone   steps up to a wooden door

smiled sadly and with morose and lachrymose lyrics into my shirt

my glasses were off   I climbed down the ditch
across from my house   through the mountain ash
around the chain-link fence   into Petersen field
toward the pitcher's mound   where I had seen
from my living room window something glint in the sunlight
on an overcast morning   after a violent shower
I bent over to look   the dark ground was unmarked
I circled around   a crow cawed

STARS

    RED

      WHITE SKY SPIN

            spin

head lolls left a weight builds on the   skull relieves
almost fall turn to see on   the road two teenagers
         blurry look now for what

hit me my head
my hair is hot. I touch it. My hand is red. The earth is bare. I don't breathe
I fly across the field   vault the fence   coat sleeve catches on
the wire tears   into the yard
the streets are mute paralysed and stupid

MOM SOMETHING HIT ME IN THE HEAD

OH my GOD!

Mom, am I going to die?
Cut two inches long. Phone my aunt the nurse. No stitches
or a hospital. No police—couldn't see. But why LORD
wasn't I wearing my glasses?

Could've been a rock or a beer bottle
bled until well past bedtime went to school
tomorrow

went back last year with my camera
everything has shrunk. Still overcast
the trailer park has rusted and sunk
got a beautiful shot of a low flying plane in black and white

the silence here rots like damp wood

DEAD
~~END~~
STREET

(runny red spray paint obscures the "END"
on a street sign in an alley in the Miller Addition,
a subdivision next to Fort George Park)

once L. and I
meet at my work, on 7th Ave.
an inter-agency social services office
where I'm head spittoon cleaner. I also service
chamber pots. L. has come to pick
up his welfare check. I pretend not to see
him, then not to recognise him. He says hi. Later
I hear that he dropped out, got addicted to crack, had three kids
by three different girls ("Hoes"/ "Bitches")

B. has got a kid, the mom pushes a carriage around
everywhere (mostly 20th Ave.) while B. rides circles around them
on his lowrider BMX. I guess he did stop selling dope
for a while

L. has gone to jail for now, I saw it in the paper
at school

the distance between the ends of our street
has grown like willows over
the graves of the ones we might bury
at opposite ends
of Prince George
Municipal Cemetery

& how will we cross those landscaped grounds
when we are inconsolable

(passing reflections on the Nechako)

in the green water rush

                              close your eyes to daylight
hard   overcast

                                                    (the sun has passed
                                                   behind a cloud

                                        sink

                waist-deep

I know   I will   wake up.   I know I will
wake up.   I know   I will
        the reeds and decayed river-life, remains of trees
wake up.
                      A death
                            red vision behind the lids.
A silent world

               unresponsive
                    / to his name

red light shocks me awake
                    / asleep .

"If you wanted to say something to someone dead, and
you prayed to God that He would tell it to them, would He, and
would they understand?"

Dear God,
       the sun has passed behind a cloud

                           dear God

Words for the memorial are words for the memory
                            I tell her
      for the mourners   she agrees
tears are for
        what (?

sure   repeat some buoyant cliché and suck in

                     (I can't write this

sink
pray anyway
      for deliverance
           for the remainder
                 this could be the rapture
in slow motion
         I told them   half-kidding
              and we wouldn't know
                    without
prophets who prophesied so
         over our newly dead
             (there'd be gnashing of teeth
and these truncated phrases
        would announce nothing
           /—nothing so clear
as a trumpet fanfare   or a shotgun report

jack-knifing on a page
      or on a breath

crumpling like a body struck down
                                        or a discard sheet
collapsing like a safety glass windshield
                                    accidental
(the sun has passed
                    behind a cloud

perhaps I prayed the wrong prayer.
When the telephone rang & we thought we knew
what happened   did we pray for the wrong soul?

She said she needed to see him to make it real
but he did not look real. He looked
                                    embalmed   waxy & white
like his own ghost. Hands folded. Shirt collar carefully covering his neck

I didn't know they'd be the last photographs anyone took
I left the shutter open longer than usual   in low light
and the result was a ghostly blur.
                        Subjects in motion
                        viewed from a fixed point
                        exposed over a few seconds
                        left unpredictable traces
                        like firecrackers going off

rejoice in these frames

rejoice in that moment that precedes the terminal
moment   rejoice
in the lack of image definition that eludes
these pictures redeem the accidental

plant posies
beneath the pavement

(black spray paint in an alley
where homeless people sleep)

from an off-white corner I break

                              the silence singing
a 60 Hz hymn. House power
                    amplified
still   below 60 dB. The noise floor
settling dust.

              A crack in a wall a wisp whisper

    a crack in a door a glow tapers
                              to a fine point
                              a knife edge
                                      walked in
                    the company of a drizzling 8:00 PM.

                              I sing
                              out of doors
                              a tape listens.
                              You are the tape.
                              This page is the tape.
                              The wheels pull the tape
                              across the heads. A record/erase head
              aligned.

From an off-white corridor
I want.   To make an impression
on the tape. A high gain
signal stamped into the magnets.
Iron filings arrayed on a strip of nylon
days & hours marshalled before the amps
from the speakers

I sing
     the waves
     on the forming puddles
     cohere and disperse
     undying. A parabolic descent

                          /

                               a raindrop dive.
                               VU meter needles fall

and don't arrive. No ripples flatline
they join the murmur
of a sound that cannot be measured
I sing into the wind
                "dark clouds a-risin'—"

no more paint p.g. ...oh well?

(patchy spray paint on the wall
of a downtown office building)

two

crow song

(side A / tape heads click into place)

from over my back fence
I can see the work of the mad window smasher

I can see the moon and the sunflowers

neighbour: "Hi"
How you doing?
neighbour: "Fine, you?"
I'm doing fine, it sure has been beautiful, hasn't it?
neighbour: "Oh yeah."

I had imagined starting from the beginning

(the walk signal is on)

the time between when I left my house and arrived
at the beginning   would've been a meditation
                a sharpening

but now I see   that to approach the beginning
            is the walk I'm on

and the flickering street lamp that never turns on or off
is the meditation

the last of the cottonwood cotton breathes
through the intersection
of 20th & Spruce

already, the sound of the heads clicking into place
and the wheels beginning to turn
and the hiss of my cassette deck
has become a weight

memory a weight that moves

a weight that rolls

the breaking ice in the Fraser
not today, but
                    in my memory

and today rolls in the Fraser

these end of September days like today,
their weight rolls over you
 the anxiety of the school day
as cold as ice rolling in the Fraser

the tape of memory   rolling over your heads

this is the Veteran's Land Act

a series of stucco duplexes with identical floor plans
and the mud path that follows the Hudsons Bay Slough:
The Heritage Trails

they run through the Veteran's Land Act
'cause they're too scared to walk

and who, having lived here, would hesitate to call themselves
a veteran?

(cars)

there are signs along the slough
the city put up signs,
                    and the vandals put up signs

the city signs say "Heritage Trails" on one side of the slough, and
"Dangerous Area—Keep Out" on the other
only the ducks swim in this water

but the orange street light leaves   where it meets
the blue of new night darkness
finds depth

a depth at the edge of objects
at the edges of leaves
of each curling leaf

and every car, every pedestrian, every bicyclist
implies a threat—
implies violence

(the train whistles from far off)

all the fire out of the fireweed now
gone to seed
along the banks of the slough

(children yell)

the water: industrial greygreen

poplar and birch

I used to bicycle through here absolutely as fast as I could.

The wet and rotting newspapers along the edges of the trail
are bright blue   and tell no news

here, where the barking night dogs
make up the words as they go

(birds chirp)

the trees on my left have broken to reveal
light off the grey water
thick reeds and
the smell of garbage

and apathy

and the day's last light on the leaves on which I walk
is ghostly bluewhite
(no, not like the newspapers—they come daily; these, nightly)

every night I dream of ghosts.   Often,
they suffocate me   *(my dead street)*

and here, the historical memorial
that was placed along the slough by the well-meaning government
was destroyed by vandals

what is this smell that is suffocating me?

Does it hurt the trees to breathe the air from the mill?

The blue night light reflects on this wide part of the slough
and all of the trees and leaves
and the bushes   the leaves on the trees and on the ground
and the gravel   and the broken branches of the bushes
all reflect   this silverblue

and I can see so little without the street lights
that I could be dreaming

(loud cars)

and Queensway seems to be the real river
light industrial and chain-link fences
I pass   to give way to where I
used to live

returning to my old street, the dimensions are all wrong.
When I was nine-years-old,
                              this street
                              this street
                              this street was as broad as my mind
and now it's narrow   and I   I walk here like a giant

(my mind weighted down)

The geography of my town is always mangled in my dreams
but the ghosts are right.

The only thing that hasn't shrunk are the trees

strange people and their cats live in my house
it looks like they've fixed the place up pretty good

              there are TVs glowing mutely through polyester curtains.
              Might as well watch a washing machine.

The weather leaves scars on the street

(two small dogs on long leashes cross the street to bark at me

a man whose face I could not see backlit by street lights
walked two small dogs past

who were very suspicious of me & my tape recorder)
a moth in the light
and I walk toward the light from the train

(camera snaps)

(the rumble of the train is loud here)

when you first look at the river,
it looks black
                            but as your eyes adjust,
you begin to see   that the river reflects the trees and the cutbanks
and the light from the train

and a car drives by too slow
while you think about   the river
and the grinding song of the train
and, scratching your unshaven face,
you get up off of the bench you sat on
with its inches of graffiti
and you notice that the car has stopped ,   at a suspicious place

and you walk down to the shore
to see   what you can see   reflected in the river

and to your left, there are long copper nails
where the lights   on the Yellowhead bridge
reflect on the water long
rippling   and drawn to a point
and the cars streak by like shooting stars in slow motion
and the rocks turn under your feet

and if there were one hour more light, you could see yourself
in the Fraser water   instead of blackness
broken by muddy stones

(train whistles close by)

and here, you can feel the weight of the river

at this distance, you can see   that the ripples that go by
on the surface of the Fraser   could carry away anything
and eventually they will

and all these industrial lines and wires   concrete scraps
and duplexes with stucco

                    will all be carried away

as you look back over the high places on the bank, through the tall grass,
you want to know: is that car still there?

And it is.
Maybe the shadows are deep enough to get away
maybe they didn't even see you

but through it all, you're not really scared

(a big loud dog barks)

a dog barks   shattering my silence

I was looking through the windows
of my old house basement   where I used to live
where we used to get the flood
the lights in the whole house are on
& the dog's bark startled me
'cause I knew I shouldn't have been looking there

wondering why I came down here (tape side abruptly ends)

(side B / tape heads pop and click)

the trails have gone cold and black

the gravel I remember has been paved over

standing on the yellow bridge

the park is silent
the cars are alive

when I looked over the yellow bridge,
I saw the flashing
of a satellite in the water
and I heard the gravel slip down the side.

When I was twelve, we used to stand on that bridge
(used to walk all through the bushes down
along the side, find change, find
magazine scraps. Maybe see owls, martens)

now I can see   nothing

and the Fraser–Fort George Museum, they turned into
the Exploration Place   covered it with lights
and filled the lobby with   taxidermy bears
frozen in aggressive poses

my South Fort has been flooded
("mine." Another white man takes
possession of this place)

                          black Fraser water
will rise over it
and maybe it'll be as I remember it

the old fire engine in Fort George Park
was dangerous   it was a real fire engine
and it was red.   And the tires had been taken off, and it had been
installed permanently in the playground

but kids slipped on it and hurt themselves. The metal ladders
were bolted down, and you could run through them
kicking your legs up over each rung
                        they cut off everything but the truck's front end.
They repainted it with flames on it.
They replaced the sand with wood chips.

The ground here still feels like flesh
the roots of trees feel like bones

(and no map indicates where the houses were exactly,
where the graveyard was exactly, and if it was
as big as the memorial, or if it was
under the playground)

(camera clicks)

and what is the difference between a ghost
and a dream about a ghost?

Then you reach a point of saturation

street lights turn on as you walk by
and there are a few feet where your steps are illuminated
you look at every corner   and every corner
every gutter runs   with memory

and you're soaked through like a rotting newspaper
on the bank of the slough

and the shoes that you expected to be hanging from the phone lines
have been cut down *(probably now walking around on strange feet)*

and the street signs you vandalised have all been replaced

and you never get lost in this neighbourhood anymore
because you know where you are.

And the gas station closed down
and the lights keep changing

and up here, coming into the light, I can see
I can see my clothes
and maybe I can even see what I couldn't see
of myself in the river

(pushing the button for a walk signal; cars go by; the signal activates:
"the walk light
                to cross Queensway
                                is on." *A metallic woman's voice.)*

Back on the other side of Queensway
my sense of time   begins to return

there's no way to go back to my old neighbourhood
because it's not there anymore

(I left for a better place.

A more central location.)

I can't deny   that over on my left
is a building that houses a tattoo parlour
and a pawnshop called "PG New & Used"
the worst part is the fact that the front railing
is made out of wagon wheels

the long grass in the vacant lot
strokes the back of my hand

(loud cars)

the life of the neighbourhood has been replaced
by the intimidating postures of new trucks on their way through

I wanted to say   I wanted to tell the story of my streets
but when I got there   they weren't

I thought I would be able to see their reflections in the river

just blurred black trees, rippling street lights, and the train

a mirror
but one that I could not see myself in

Thursday night's good for watching television
but the doors of the Connaught Youth Centre are strangely open

(trumpets)

inside   a squadron of air cadets stands at attention
and here the Greyhound bus rolls by
carrying another busload of people into Parkwood Place

(walk signal)

and here at 17th and Victoria is where they put up the sign that claims
that this is called the Gateway

in giant letters, someone spray-painted "the fairies"
on a white wall   but it's been painted over

and here again, I can see all the corporate logos
and with the corporate logos come the minivans

and this is where I want to go

(bustle of a busy intersection)

and now, more than ever, I am back in the light
where kids push each other around in a big barren parking lot
in stolen Value Village shopping carts
and everyone wanders around in baseball caps

and the crow song is silent

(a woman is talking about writing
laughter "take me home, quick!" laughter
"well, if you really want to get over the embarrassment,
do a mall signing" laughter
"you're faced with this onslaught of people" laughter
"the most common question you're asked is
'have you seen my husband?'" laughter

tape clicks out)

pause to pretend to be polite

(chairs clatter in front of a café, people talk, cars start)

(muffled, talking to Rob)

...I don't have much time left,
and that's good...

...by the time I walked down to Paddlewheel Park,
it was black out...

...it's just dark, like a memory you can't really have...

...the more corporate logos, the more people...

Rob: "Our new next-door neighbour came by to say
they were so glad we had kids...   ...making some noise...
...heard them playing in the back yard..."

...So, when I play this tape back, I'm not even sure, what I'm going to...

Rob: "I had this pedal that I used for transcribing interviews..."

...Well, my mom has been a professional secretary for...

…I don't think that's an exclusive thing, though…

Rob: "What you might do though, is instead of doing a faithful transcription, use it as a starting point to write off of…"

…Oh, that's a good idea…you know, my Prince George has moved so much, I'm concerned (tape abruptly ends)

acknowledgements

The "passing reflections on the Nechako" section is for Bruce Dempster. The pieces that begin "once L. and I" are all for L. W. Some of the poems in this book appeared in the chapbook *one hour more light* (wink books, 2004).

Thanks to all the writers whose words and works have influenced and encouraged me. Thanks to my family and friends. Thanks to Rob Budde for his editorial contributions and to Jake Kennedy for his. Thanks to Vici, Erin S. and all the folks at Caitlin who helped make this book happen. A special thanks to Erin, my partner: these poems would be lonely without you.